Praise for Alan ten-Hoeve:

"*Notes from a Wood-Paneled Basement* made me feel how I did the first time I saw *The 400 Blows*. A poignant sadness hangs in the air of this poetry collection, but then such wonder grabs your collar and takes you sprinting to the sea. Punk rock, stink bugs, the last good memory from childhood. Alan ten-Hoeve is a wonderful poet."

—Bud Smith, author of *Double Bird* and *Teenager*

"With pieces filled with pathos and wit and work rooted in connection and working-class honesty, *Notes from a Wood-Paneled Basement* looks at what we do with our time, our memories, the complicated pictures of our parents that come into clearer focus the older we get. It squares what we inherited against what we refuse to pass on and asks whether we can enjoy the tiny/funny/happy/sad moments that are, slowly, becoming our life. Simply put, Alan ten-Hoeve is one of the few writers I'd read anything from, and *Notes from a Wood-Paneled* Basement is one of the best books I've read in a very long time. An absolutely stunning debut."

—Nick Olson, EIC of (mac)ro(mic) and author of *Here's Waldo* and *The Brother We Share*

"Bah-gawd, that's Alan ten-Hoeve's music!! *Notes from a Wood-Paneled Basement* delivers a Stone Cold Stunner straight to the heart. But before it does that, it proceeds to smash two beers against its forehead and flip you off. All in good fun, of course. Alan's poetry is a masterclass in honesty, bursting at the seams with pop culture references and humor. TL;DR: put this collection in your pipe and smoke it, baby."

—Shawn Berman, editor of *The Daily Drunk* and author of *Mr. Funnyman*

"Some of these poems were pretty good."

—Poe Ballantine, author of *Love & Terror on the Howling Plains of Nowhere*

Alan ten-Hoeve's

Notes from
a Wood-Paneled Basement

*To Coleman,
Proud to be your press mate. Hope you dig.
HtN*

Gob Pile Press
SE Ohio

GOB PILE PRESS

First Edition: Copyright © 2021 Alan ten-Hoeve

All rights reserved. No part of this work may be reproduced in any way without written permission from the author except small excerpts for review.

Cover photo: Alan ten-Hoeve

Design/layout: Bram Riddlebarger

@gobpilepress

gobpilepress@gmail.com

www.gobpilepress.bigcartel.com

GPP004

ISBN: 9798465261906

For Ashley, Arlo, Hazel, and Billy

NOTES FROM
A WOOD-PANELED BASEMENT

Punk

Me and a few friends got into punk during high school.
Misfits, Dead Kennedys, Black Flag, Minor Threat, Minutemen, Bad Brains.
Shit like that.

To separate ourselves from the
preps,
the jocks,
and the thugs we
dressed in ripped jeans, Chucks, and punk t-shirts.
Shaved our heads.
Gave each other hand pokes with India ink and walked around with the shittiest fucking attitude
like we were the only ones
who suffered.

Doing our best to
fit the mold.

It took me many years to realize
that the lone girl who
wore the shit kickers
and Billy Ray Cyrus t-shirts
was more punk
than I could ever be.

To Be Continued

My parents they
lived nowhere to go lives.

Nights without dreams lives.

Drive seven days a week
to jobs without benefits or
sick pay lives.

Beat out frustration on each other lives.

Smoke cigarettes in front of the TV at four a.m.
lives.

Can't afford a doctor lives.

Look out the cloudy window of
a plywood shack
wondering if they'll make the rent lives.

All within a belief system that
can't exist without them
but won't let them live
lives.

Lives that took everything
until they died broke and broken.

Then it was my turn.

A Period at the End

Down in the basement
listening to Megadeth
as a domestic storm
rages upstairs,
sending cobwebs and
clouds of dust
raining down on my head
and scaring the mice
in the walls.

I turn up the volume.
The music blends with the
pounding,
with the vibrations, and the
weed,
sending shivers up my spine
that
ricochet in my skull.

Stoic faces in the
wood paneling
watch over me like dark wizards,
as Dave Mustaine shreds and
bends
every screaming note
and
riff.

There are many things outside
of this room
waiting to grind me down,
like work,
mortgage,

covid,
murder hornets,
politics,
my children's mental health,
and
that meme of Dave
playing a slug
instead of his guitar.

But
I'm not going to think about them
right now.
At least,
not until I

finish

this

poem

and put

a

period

at

the

Agaric Haiku

for Bram Riddlebarger

running through the yard
girl kicks yellow agarics
death comes to us all

Bullet

Dad tells me to close my eyes and hold out my hand. Something small and heavy and cold drops into my palm. When I open my eyes I see it's a bullet.

"Superman gave it to me," he says. "I was working near the top of the Empire State Building, putting in some new rivets on the outside when my harness snapped. From that height I knew I was as good as dead. Wouldn't be nothin lefta me but a pile of hot mush on West Thirty-Fourth Street."

"Were you scared?"

Dad hitches at his belt but it stays trapped beneath his belly. "Not really. We all gotta go sometime. I closed my eyes and braced for impact. But at the last second I felt something grab me. When I opened my eyes I saw it was Superman. His red cape rippling out behind him. We landed in an alley, and I thanked him for saving my life. Before flying away he said he knows you're his biggest fan and wanted you to have something."

"The bullet?"

Dad nods. "Someone tried to shoot him but he caught it midair."

"Like in the movie!"

"Just like the movie."

I look at the bullet. I don't know enough to see it has never been fired from a gun. A live round. "Was he big?"

Dad makes his hand flat, raises it a few inches above his own head. "But listen," he says and takes my chin in his hand. "Superman said don't tell your mother. She wouldn't understand. She doesn't believe in Superman. This is a secret between you, me, and him."

I know I'm not supposed to keep secrets from mom. But I figure if Superman wants me to keep a secret it must be okay. It's my duty.

I carry the bullet everywhere I go. I even bring it to school. At first it stays in the small pocket of my JanSport. But it's hard to take out and look at that way. Eventually I just keep it in the pocket of my pants. Where I can reach in and touch it anytime. When I ask to be excused to the bathroom I close myself in a stall and take it out. Polish it with my shirt. Watch the light streak down its silvery side.

I want to show the bullet to my friends. When they bring in their expensive toys they think are so great I'm tempted to take the bullet out. Who can top a gift from Superman? But I know I'm not supposed to. And even though I know I shouldn't, it gets the best of me.

One day, as we're getting our books and

homework out for our next subject, Nick, the kid who sits behind me, is talking about how his dad is taking him on a rafting trip during summer. In the Grand Canyon. Nick always brags about doing cool stuff with his dad.

And I can't take it anymore.

I slide the bullet from my pocket, turn around and open my fist. Nick's eyes go wide. His mouth falls open. He's surprised. And it feels good. But before I can tell him the story about how Superman gave it to my dad to give to me he points at my face and blurts out, "Miss Reilly, he brought a bullet to school!"

Everyone stops what they are doing. Every pair of eyes stare at me. I've never seen my teacher look so pale. Without a word she takes the bullet from my open hand. She holds it up pinched between her thumb and forefinger and looks at it as if she can't believe what she is seeing. The room is so quiet.

I'm brought to the principal's office by my elbow. I try to lie. Tell her I found the bullet outside of school. In the grass by a tree. The principal takes me outside. Makes me show her where. I chose a tree at random and point at it. She doesn't believe my story.

My mom is called in to school. She is not happy about having to leave work. In the principal's office I tell her the same lie about the tree. She doesn't say much. I think she believes me. But when we get into the car she doesn't start it right away. Instead she lights a cigarette. Says she wants to know where I *really* got the bullet.

I hesitate to answer and then she is yelling. Her voice impossibly loud inside the car. I try to hold tight to my story, just like Superman wants. But I'm not strong enough. I'm no man of steel. I burst into tears and tell her everything. When I am done she sits back and stares at me a moment before starting the car.

"Please don't tell dad I told you."

Mom doesn't say anything. She crushes out her cigarette and lights another. She puts the car in DRIVE. We go straight home without talking, my breath hitching in my chest the whole way. At home I am sent to my room where I stay for the rest of the afternoon and night.

The next day is a Saturday. When my dad comes to pick me up for visitation, mom tells me to stay in my room. My stomach hurts. I hear shouting through my closed door.

"What were you thinking!" I hear. "It hasn't even been fired it's a fuckin *live round!*"

"Jeez, fuckin relax, will ya? Stop being a bitch."

"You tell him there's no such thing as Superman!"

"The fuck I will."

They both shout over each other. Curses ring out like gunshots. Feet scuffle on kitchen tile. Chairs scrape. Something falls over and breaks. The shouts are replaced by worse sounds. I'm nauseous. Tears blur my vision. My throat hurts. I press myself into a corner. Knees to chest. Hands over ears.

I wonder where Superman is now. I could use his help.

Tuba Luba

At my wife's grandfather's
retirement community,
there's a woman who goes
by the nickname
Tuba Luba.

A kind and
generous woman, Tuba Luba
once invited us over
to her unit
for a home-cooked dinner
with lots of wine
and beer.
She even gave our kids
toys to play with
so we could concentrate
on more important things

—like getting drunk.

"Parents need to
kick back and
relax," Tuba Luba winked,
and handed my wife's grandfather
another ice cold can
of Budweiser.

Though quite curious, my
wife and I never asked
Tuba Luba her real name,
feeling it would be
impolite to pry.
But

later on,
when my wife asked her
grandfather
how the woman got such
an unusual
moniker,
he smirked and said,

"Because

—*that's* what it takes."

"They're after the place. They don't know why, they just remember. Remember that they want to be in here."
—*Dawn of the Dead* (1978)

Laundry in the Time of Covid

Eight months into this pandemic,
I sometimes wonder if anyone
bothers to fold their laundry
anymore.

To spend all our
time at home and
not see many people
besides one's family makes
the chore seem pointless.

I mean, who has time to worry
about neat, wrinkle-free clothes
when there's an apocalypse going on?

In my house
we've taken to leaving the clean clothes
in the laundry baskets and
dig things out as needed.

Sometimes I'll get up and fold, but
on these rare occasions
I can't shake the feeling that
by performing this task
I am no different than one of those
zombies
from *Dawn of the Dead*

who mindlessly return to the mall,
so enslaved to consumerism
that the habit of shopping endures
even after death,
performing actions that have somehow
been rendered even more
useless
than in our previous lives.

You Say Tomato, I Say Traumatic Bonding

Castaway
starring Tom Hanks
is the story of a man who
after a lifetime of tedium
accidentally
finds paradise.

Tragically,
due to a severe case of
PTSD
and a distaste for seafood,
he forsakes his best
friend
and risks everything
to rejoin civilization

like a
beaten spouse who
returns again and again
to their abuser.

This One

They come in drunk, try not to make too much noise stumbling through the dark single-wide. They think I'm asleep, but I am only pretending. I was up right before I saw the headlights sweep across the fake wood paneling of the living room walls. That's when I turned off the *Cheers* rerun I was watching and ran to my room.

It is long past my bedtime.

They whisper loudly and giggle like little children. I try to place the man's voice but can't. He might be new.

Through my thin walls I hear them collapse onto the pullout couch. The springs and rickety metal frame start creaking. Giggles and whispers give way to other noises. I pull my Walkman from under my bed, put on the headphones, and hit play. "Control" by Janet Jackson fills my ears, the only cassette I own. I crank the volume as loud as it goes but can't completely drown out my mother. I wish she would have taken the bedroom and given me the pullout in the living room. That's where the TV is.

In the morning I wake up with my headphones still on and the pillow over my head. Leaving my room, I find the two of them passed out, their bodies twisted in dirty sheets. The man is completely naked, his schlong hangs limp like an old, wrinkled hotdog. I don't recognize this one, but it's hard to be sure. They always seem to have the same kind of mustache.

Tiptoe to the kitchen.

Most of her boyfriends ignore me, looking awkward and anxious to leave as they smoke their morning cigarettes at the kitchen table. Some stick around longer than others. A few try to be pals. I prefer the ones who ignore me.

One time, a guy named Bill took me to see wrestling. That was okay. We had third row seats by the aisle where I got high-fives from Tito Santana, Rockin' Robin, and my hero, Hulk Hogan. The memory gives me a little hope. Maybe this one won't be so bad either.

I eat cereal beside the pull-out on the living room floor, watch Wrestling Challenge on channel five while they sleep off their hangovers.

When this one finally wakes up, he is bleary-eyed and confused at my presence, at where he is. Looking around the room and down at my sleeping mother, realization slowly settles on his face. He focuses on the TV, and sneers.

"Hey kid. You know that shit is fake, right?"

Flock Blocked

While watching a flock of birds
on the deck this
morning
our cat, Billy, launched herself
for an attack,
forgetting
all about the
sliding screen door
separating her
from them.

It's not the first
time
she's done that.

I wonder if the birds
find this as
funny as I do.

Measuring One's Mortality through Aging Teen Movies

Adventures in Babysitting is on HBO,

followed by *Blue Crush*.

Adventures in Babysitting

was released in nineteen eighty-seven.

Blue Crush in two thousand two.

I never saw *Blue Crush*

but

think of it as a movie that

isn't from so long ago.

Yet it's older than

Adventures in Babysitting was

when *it* was released.

Sometimes I think about that stuff.

Broken Record

I've said it before
and I'll say it
til I'm blue in the face:

Some Kind of Monster
and
Mean Girls are
basically the same movie.

I'm so Hungry I Could Eat out the Ass End of a Dead Rhino

I was down in the basement
wrestling
with the word and
getting my ass kicked
when
I heard loud,
booming laughter
coming from upstairs.

Sometimes,
genius spills forth like a
geyser and
there's nothing I can do
to stop it.

Other times it
has to be teased
like a limp dick, and
I need peace and quiet.

This night was a
limp dick.

I went up to
see what the hell and
found my wife on the living room couch
watching
Point Break on HBO.
She was contorted with hysterics.

"What the shit?" I said. "What's so

funny?"

"This movie," she guffawed. "Are these really . . .

the best takes . . .

they could get?"

I hadn't seen *Point Break* in
years, but
it was one of my favorites growing up.

It existed in my memory as a great
action movie,
featuring badass surfing outlaws
who robbed banks disguised in
rubber
ex-president masks, and
the cool FBI agent who
goes undercover to
apprehend them.

I remembered it as a subversive
and
morally ambiguous film about
meeting one's dark side,
filled with dramatic, adrenaline-
pumping chase scenes,
rock star cameos,
shootouts,
skydiving,
and,
of course,
nudity.

It had everything to appeal to a
teenage me.
I'd seen it many times.

I didn't remember it being
very funny.

Except for that line
about the dead rhino's ass.

Looking at the TV, I
saw it was at the part where
Gary Busey gets shot at the airport.
Keanu Reeves,
looking handsomely
anguished,
screams, "No! No!"
Then runs over and,
awkwardly using his entire
palm,
checks for a pulse that
isn't there
by slapping his
dead partner's neck.

Seeing this, my wife fell into another
peal of laughter.

"Jeez! Keep it down," I said,

"you're gonna wake the kids."

Every Time Someone Mentions That Band You Played with Once Who Got Famous

for Zac Smith

"Did I tell you Zac Smith tweeted something about guitar tone and playing style on that first Yeah Yeah Yeahs album?"

"Who's Zac Smith?"

"You know they stole that sound from my old band, right? We played a show with them in Brooklyn before they were famous and I know there was cross-pollination. Their song "Maps" is a complete rip-off of our song "Atlas" which is like, four years older. And don't even get me started on how Karen O stole our singer's moves."

[rubbing their face]: "Yes, I've heard something about that before."

"And Zac wrote a friggin' article about it. It's not even true."

"Was it a tweet or an article."

"It's a book. About how the Yeah Yeah Yeahs invented sound. Netflix has optioned it for a four-part limited series."

"We should watch that."

"Yeah?"

"Yeah."

"Yeah."

A Nice Day at the Park

The grandparents on my dad's side brought me. Grooty and Opa. And I had this little wooden wagon. I'd won it in a raffle during a kindergarten fundraiser. When the teacher pulled the ticket and called my name I sat there frozen, unable to believe I had won. Someone had to nudge me forward to claim my prize.

The wagon was red. Had sides that could be removed. Wheels that turned whichever way I pulled the handle. "The Cadillac of wagons," Opa called it. It was my most favorite thing in the world.

I pulled the wagon around the park. Its red paint gleamed in the sun. I filled it with rocks, sticks, and lots of litter: styrofoam coffee cups, candy wrappers, paper bags, twist tops, bottles. Whatever I could find. Then I'd roll the wagon over to another spot, remove a side and spill everything out like a dump truck.

During one of my trips to the trash heap, a little girl about my age with braids and pink bow-shaped berets appeared in front of me. She wore a plaid outfit with buttoned shoulder straps and ugly shoes. Her hands clasped behind her back. She asked if she could ride in the wagon.

I'd never seen this girl before. She was a stranger. The cop who visited my classroom told us not to talk to strangers. I felt nervous, but I was also bored of playing with myself.

I looked over at my grandparents for some sign of approval. That it'd be okay this one time. Opa was reading the newspaper, smoke trailing from the pipe clamped in his dentures. Grooty was talking to another old lady in a similar house dress who had even more warts than her. A woman I didn't recognize. A stranger.

I dumped out the load where I stood and the little girl climbed in my wagon. We took turns pulling each other. The tires sank into the wood chips on the playground and got stuck. It was easier on the grass. Easier still on the walking path, where runners and cyclists made annoyed faces and sounds when they had to swerve around us.

We did this for a long time. Until our families called us to go home. I can't remember who left first. Me, or the girl.

Back at my grandparents' house, Grooty made us scrambled eggs. Opa ate his with herring. I had mine with crumb cake Opa bought fresh from the bakery that morning.

As I was eating the crumbs off the top of my cake, Grooty started talking about our time at the park. How nice it was to see so-and-so again, how nice the weather was.

Opa shoved eggs in his mouth. Flecks of

herring clung to his greasy lips. He slurped at his glass of Coke.

Grooty turned to me, said, "And what was your little friend's name?"

"I don't know."

Grooty smiled. "Well, it was very nice of you to play with that little girl even though she was black."

Grooty had a thick North Jersey accent that made her sound like Olive Oyl from the Popeye cartoons. When she said the word *girl* it came out like *goil*.

"You sound like Olive Oyl," I said.

I watched Grooty get up. Rinse her plate under the faucet and stare out the window over the sink. "It really is a beautiful day," she said.

Opa said nothing.

My eggs were turning cold.

Unwinding Haiku

more holes appear
in the hull each day
stars at twilight

The Night My Father's Fiancé Came to Dinner

I think it would make her happy if you called her 'Mother,' he said.

But she isn't my Mother.

He grabbed my arm and jerked.

You will call her 'Mother.'

I did.

Lost Ticket

Early Sunday mornings
I'd turn the dial and adjust the rabbit ears to see
what channels came in.
The one with the preacher
was always clearest,
like God himself
controlled the airwaves.

The preacher wore a stuffy suit,
dabbed his face with a handkerchief
and blathered about God as
a toll-free number flashed on the screen below.
One morning I was listening to him go on and on
about sin and how God will forgive me
no matter what I say or do.
He started listing off all the many ways we piss off God.
Spit flew from his lips.
He waved his arms and staggered weak-
kneed from one side of the stage
to the other. As if
just speaking these things
drained him of redemption.
As the preacher's rant was hitting its peak,
he paused,
repeated that God would
forgive me no matter what
but added, "Except for this one thing."

This was something I'd never heard
before.

Usually he just said
all I had to do was ask for God's forgiveness,
and for a donation,
I shall have it.

The preacher stared into the camera,
into my eyes, into
my soul,
his face slick with sweat he
didn't bother to wipe away.
He raised his pointer finger and said
if I did this one thing, if—
if I committed this one sin
it would surely get me nothing
but a one-way ticket to Hell,
and,
just as he was about to tell me what
this one thing
not even God almighty could forgive was,
I reached out and
snapped off the TV.

I didn't want to hear it.

I knew I'd be tempted to do whatever it was
I wasn't supposed to
do.
Little did I know
I'd endure many Hells
regardless.

Now older and hopefully
wiser, I
regret not waiting around to hear
what the TV preacher had to say

all those years ago,
because now I have no way to know
if I've committed this
ultimate sin, if I've
reserved my ticket to Hell
or not.
But I suppose that's no reason
to quit trying. It's
best
to be sure.

Piñata

My seven-year-old daughter sits at the kitchen table, covers a small, inflated balloon with papier mâché, then sets it outside to dry.

I don't ask what she is doing. I am too concerned with things going on in the world outside of our home to notice.

When the papier mâché dries, she paints it with different colors, including a section of leopard print.

I move through the house like a ghost. Not seeing. Not hearing. Not really here.

Popping the balloon inside, she fills the colorful shell with lollipops, sour warheads, and pinwheel mints, then tells everyone we are invited to a party.

I am annoyed to take time away from my worrying, my frustration, my anger—the knowledge that I cannot fix what is truly broken.

The four of us go outside by the tree swing where my daughter produces a box of face paints.

"Who wants their face painted," she says and her mom volunteers.

My twelve-year-old strings the little piñata

from a branch. I pace with my arms folded across my chest, waiting for it to be over.

Using a yellow Wiffle ball bat, we take turns swinging. The piñata turns out to be quite thick and sturdy.

I swat flies from my face, slap at a few mosquitos, and stew in my foul mood as I go through the motions.

My wife, her face painted like a cat, delivers the final blow.

The piñata breaks.

Candy flies through the air

and scatters in the weeds.

The kids run to gather it up.

I go inside before the last piece is found, so consumed with my dark thoughts that I never notice how much fun everyone had for a few minutes.

Later, my daughter tells me I didn't take my goodie bag and hands me a paper bag decorated with planets. It is filled with stickers, a pin with a bear on it, some bracelets she made, a finger puppet, dental floss, and a drawing of me.

Hating myself for so many reasons, I go to

stick the pin on the pocket flap of an old jacket.
At the same moment I pierce the flannel
material, I break open,

guts spill out like candy from a busted piñata.

I fall to my knees and begin the process

of stuffing it all back in.

Hard Times

Sometimes
it's best to
drop everything
and
play *Mario Kart*
with the kids.

Spring Rain Scene

A lone turkey
emerges
from its hiding place
in the woods.

I watch at my
kitchen window as
it high steps around pale,
unfurling skunk cabbage
and
crosses the swollen
drainage ditch.

Rain rolling off
oily feathers, it
scratches at
wet leaves
looking for something
to eat.

Finding nothing
the turkey moves on.

I want to follow the turkey,
go somewhere else too.

I chose another cup of coffee
instead.

43% Burnt Chickadee

The chickadee
outside my window
sounds like a
Dillinger Escape Plan song.

Dee-dee-dee-dee
Chicka
Dee-dee-dee-dee-dee

Dee-dee-dee-dee
Chicka
Dee-dee-dee-dee

Dee-dee-dee-dee

Chicka
Dee-dee-dee
Chicka
Dee-dee-dee-dee

Chicka
Dee-dee-dee-dee-dee

Sun Shower

The humid heat of the day
allayed by a brief sun-shower.

Puddles reflect light
on my bedroom ceiling

as steam rises
off the back deck.

Bucket of Fish

On Friday we go to the town lake.
Bring our fishing rods and tackle box.
A container of worms from the garden.

I bait the hooks.
We quickly break our record.
Catch like fourteen or fifteen sunnies and one lake trout.
I take pictures of my youngest holding hooked bodies wriggling on the line.
I think maybe some of the fish are caught more than once.
Unable to resist the hunks of juicy, quivering worm.

Some have spots and bright orange bellies.
The fish, not the worms.
We put a few in a bucket filled with water.
Watch them swim in circles.
Look for a way out.
Give up.

The swallows we've seen fly in and out of the drainpipes under the overpass aren't around as they were the last time we were here.
The storm must have washed their nests and babies away.

A group of people arrive with paddle boards.
Between casts we watch them paddle out on the lake.
When we look up one time they are gone. Out of sight.

Probably swallowed by the lake monster.

We tried fishing the pond in town a few times.
But there didn't seem to be any fish there.
And the water grass at the edge was tall and thick.
Every cast got snagged or tangled.

The sun rises over the trees.
Lifeguards start to show up to the lake.
Teenagers with summer jobs.
They look so young I can't imagine them saving someone's life.
I vaguely remember a kid drowning here years ago.

People soon arrive carrying beach chairs, towels, and coolers.
We pour the bucket of fish back into the lake.
The paddle boarders haven't come back.

And People Say There's Nothing to Do around Here

At a fair in small town America, people
descend on games and junk food.

A cover band provides a soundtrack to the
feeding.

Arriving home that evening,
fairgoers collapse on their couches,
a little fatter for the slaughter.

Tenacity

Our cat
hasn't caught a mouse
in weeks

yet she still keeps
a nightly vigil
near the hole.

Two Frost Haiku

for Chris La Tray

frost dusting the trees
cat sleeps on radiator
winter is coming

pink morning sunlight
sparkles on the frosty grass
crunch beneath my boots

The Night Life

I often wake up early,
hours before the sun,
and pace the inside of my head.

It doesn't take long before
dreary thoughts begin to intrude,
to
pollute the stillness.

I sit up,
prop on the edge of the mattress,
then
slide off.

Feet on the chilly floor,
I step to the bedroom window,
look at the stars,
at the
long moonlit shadows of trees
laying across a snowy ground
littered
with animal tracks.

Everything is so quiet out here
in the country,
it seems the world
has died.

An owl calls
through the darkness,
as if to reassure me, and
the whoosh of the furnace is there, too,
then the clank of the radiator

as hot steam fills the old pipes.

I used to live in tiny apartments
in cities where drunks
and addicts
roamed the streets outside, and
I could hear the neighbors
fight through the thin walls,
stomp overhead,
scream
with the insanity of the world,
as cockroaches and mice
had parties in the dark.

The night life might have been
more interesting back then,
but
I think I like it here
better

don't I?

Test

I have trouble
sleeping at night,

during the day I can
drop off almost anytime.

But at night
it feels like a test,

and I choke.

So I lay there
doing nothing.

Hoping that
sleep will come.

Hours will go by as I
stare at the shadows on the wall.
At the cracks in the ceiling.

Listen
to a lone car
drifting over the rumble strip
in the middle of
the road.

Or my wife
mumbling in her sleep.

I'm afraid to get up, afraid
to move.

Our house is small and the
slightest noise is liable
to wake people up.

But my bladder is full.

I walk to the bathroom
try to be quiet
to avoid the creaky
floorboards
but
fail every time.

At least I don't
stub my toe or
step on any abandoned toys
this time.

I piss in the bowl
just above the water line.

Don't flush.

I stare in the mirror and
play with my graying beard.

On the way back
to my room I
shoo the cat from the counter and
see my young daughter.

She stands in the
doorway of her bedroom
rubbing her eyes.

She tells me I
am being too noisy.

I am often impatient with her
putting my own needs first and
tonight I feel the heavy guilt
of my faults.

I tuck her into bed
under the Elsa and Anna sleeping bag
she uses as a blanket
then
return to my own room
where I stare at the
shadows
and listen
as she sings herself
back to sleep.

Dream Piano

My wife sleeps peacefully beside me
curled in a thick blanket
uttering little sounds, little
transmissions from dreamland.

Her fingers
twitch against my arm and
I imagine she is playing
a dream piano.

A mouse
scratches inside the wall.

Commitment

Seriously
thinking
about
cutting
the
tags
off
these
basketball
shorts.

The Squared Circle

When I was a little boy,
my
dad would often take me
to a local arena that
held regular WWF events.

We spent so many
hours
watching men and women
battle inside the squared circle
and sometimes out.

At one such event,
I noticed something I
hadn't noticed before
and thought about what I'd heard
one of mom's boyfriends
say about
wrestling.

During intermission,
as the crowd dispersed to
buy food,
beer,
and
t-shirts,
I asked my dad if
wrestling was real.

He looked at me earnestly,
put a hand on my
shoulder, and said,

Yes son, it is.

It wasn't the
worst lie
he ever told.

At a Red Light in Nineteen Eighty-Three

I was sitting in the
passenger seat of my dad's pickup,
waiting for the light to turn green
when a couple crossed in-
front of us.
They were holding hands and
being affectionate in public.

One of them was
light-skinned,
the other dark.

As we watched them go,
dad turned the radio down,
and told me,
"Blacks and whites, they
can't have babies together.
Their blood can't mix.
The baby's blood will be dirty."

"Does the baby die?"

Dad pressed his lips
together.
"Sometimes," he said.
"A doctor can try to
drain all the baby's blood and
put clean blood in.
But it doesn't always work."

The couple moved out of sight.
The light turned green.
We rolled through the intersection.

"What about Chinese people?" I said.
"And Spanish people. Can
they have babies with
different colored people?"

My dad thought about it a minute.
"That could be okay
since they're not as dark.
But I wouldn't.
Just to be safe."

I nodded.
"Where do babies come from?"

Dad shot me a side glance
before quickly returning his eyes
to the windshield.

"That's not important
right now.
Just remember
what I told you."

I looked out the window.

Watched the world go by.

"Okay,"
I said.

"I won't forget."

The Ram-bo

Dave comes over my house. Shows me an archery set he got for his twelfth birthday. The bow is sleek and black with pulleys on the ends. Like the one his idol, Rambo, has. Dave says it's called a compound bow. A Rambo Bow. The pulleys give it more power. More distance. He pulls back the string and aims at an imaginary enemy. I am jealous.

There is a strut to Dave's step as we stalk bushes in the neighborhood and keep an eye out for the NVA. Dave wears camo and a red bandana tied around his head. The bow slung across his back with an arrow holder he calls a quiver. Which I think is a funny word to call something.

If no one is watching, Dave shoots arrows at tree trunks or sets up some trash for targets. He recites Rambo as he sneaks up on the enemy:

"I'll give you a war you won't believe."

"You're not hunting me, I'm hunting you."

"To survive a war, you gotta become war."

After loosing an arrow at an enemy cereal box or milk container, he looks at me, curls his lip, and in a low, gravely voice says, "They drew first blood, not me. They drew first blood."

When Dave tries to kill a squirrel, it is too fast. It arcs across the top of a fence. Leaps into a tree and disappears in the branches. He misses every shot.

Gathering the arrows, Dave tells me he's going to join the army the day he turns eighteen. That that will be his birthday gift to himself. And his country. He wants to be a Green Beret. "A hero." Keep America free. He says most people think the Marines are the best, or the Navy Seals, but really it's the Green Berets. Dave's dad was in the army. So were his uncles and grandfathers. He has relatives buried in Arlington, whatever that means. A military family.

My Uncle Carmine says that war is just poor people killing each other for rich people. Uncle Carmine protested the Vietnam War when he was young. Now he comes to family barbecues and tells us military people are shitheads. No mind of their own. Fascists and bullies and wannabes who do as they are told without asking why or caring if it's right. Sacrificing their lives and the lives of others for nothing. The opposite of heroes.

But I don't bring it up to Dave.

I want a turn with his bow and arrows.

Sometimes Dave lets me take a few shots. He shows me how to nock an arrow. How to use the sights to aim. Other times, usually after he misses his targets, he'll claim he has to get home when I ask for a turn. Or he'll glance around dramatically and say something like, "I think I heard someone. It doesn't feel safe."

A few days after getting the archery set, Dave and I are walking past the town park, looking for something new to shoot at, something more interesting than trees and garbage. The place is empty. Not a soul in sight. Dave stops by the playground fence and stares out into the distance as the wind plays with his wispy rattail.

I follow his eyes. Try to see what he sees. "What?"

Dave slips the bow from his shoulder, jerks his chin yonder, across the field used for soccer and baseball games. "Go see where it lands."

I hesitate. Dave sees the look on my face and curls his lip. Quotes his hero. "Don't worry. In the field we had a code of honor: You watch my back, I watch yours."

Something in my young idiot brain tries to tell me this isn't a good idea, but I ignore that and run across the field anyway. It's a long way. I have plenty of time to reconsider.

When I get to the other side, huffing and puffing, I wave that I am ready. Dave looks tiny from where I stand. I hear him yell something, but it gets carried away in the wind. Some kind of Rambo howl. Then miniature Dave nocks an arrow, pulls back the string as far as it goes, angles it up, and lets go.

At the last second, I feel scared I won't be able to see the arrow. That my eyes will lose it against the sky or the sun will blind me and the arrow will come down and impale me through a vital organ, nick an artery, or go through an eye, maybe stab me in the dick.

But it's an overcast day, and I can follow the slim, bright orange line against the steel gray clouds with ease. I watch it rise high into the sky, higher than I would have imagined it could fly, and I think, *Damn, that bow has power*.

As I try to gauge where the arrow will come down and stick in the field, I realize something is wrong. I shade my eyes and watch the arrow soar high over my head. Over the basketball court and parking lot behind me. Toward a cul-de-sac beyond. I see the arrow pierce the aluminum siding of a house. Stick at an angle just below an open second story window. A loud *pop* reaches my ears a half second later.

I stand there amazed and dumbfounded at how far the arrow traveled and where it is now stuck. Another inch or two up and—a man's head and torso appear in the window. He looks at the arrow. Then at me. His face changes from disbelief to anger. "Hey, you! Stay right there!"

"But I didn't do anything."

"Stay right there!"

"I didn't do anything."

The man's torso slips back inside. It occurs to me I should probably get out of there.

When I turn to run back across the field, Dave is already gone.

Holiday Shopping with Dad

He dragged me from the store in a headlock.

My little sneakers squeaking on the floor for purchase.

All you care about is your damn mother, was all he said.

Through pain and tears I saw store employees staring.

It was deathly quiet as my skull strained against its sutures.

Bitchin' Sideburns

July third, two thousand three

I was at the Hammerstein Ballroom to see Foo Fighters/My Morning Jacket/Pete Yorn.

Standing in line with a friend to buy overpriced beers, a couple of ladies in front of us did a double take at me and said, "You look familiar."

Before I could respond, my friend said, "He's Alan Yorn, Pete's younger brother."

He said this without any hesitation, as if he'd practiced this very line before.

To my surprise the ladies didn't question this even though the only resemblance I shared with the singer, as far as I could tell, were a pair of bitchin' sideburns.

Less Flat

Standing on the corner under the maple tree, where the grass is still damp from a morning rain. Moisture seeps into my worn-out sneakers.

I watch the cars go by, then hear the familiar sound of the school bus cresting the hill. It emerges into view with lights flashing, first yellow, then red.

When my five-year-old daughter steps down through the folding doors, she holds the whole world in her hand.

Two round pieces of paper, an eastern and western hemisphere, taped together with crumpled paper stuffed inside to make it "less flat."

She has used crayons to make the paper earth's water dark blue, and each continent, labeled in her awkward handwriting, is shaded with a different color.

At school, her class is learning about geography.

She smiles as a cool breeze tosses her hair, and gives me her free hand, to hold as we walk to the driveway.

UFO

He shows me a fuzzy picture of a bright red oval-shaped line in a sea of blackness.

"What is it?"

Dad makes a face like I should know. "It's a UFO," he says. "Fuckin' aliens! I took the picture a couple weeks ago and just got it developed. I wanted to make sure I got it before I told you."

It's a sleepover visitation weekend. We'd spent the afternoon at the wrestling matches, then went to the bar across the street from his apartment for liverwurst sandwiches and Shirley Temples. We ate at a table by the tinted window, under a neon sign that said COLD BEER but was off during the day. That's when he pulled out the picture.

"Do you think it'll come back?" I feel scared but also exhilarated. Like when he has me hold those little firecrackers so he can light the fuse with the tip of his cigarette. One time I didn't throw it fast enough, and I went to the hospital with burns on my fingers.

"I don't know . . . maybe."

I don't have a room at dad's apartment. I sleep on the couch. It's a couch with weird black fabric that feels like fur. I call it Fur Couch. When I run my hand over the fur one way, it is shiny and black. If I go the other way, it is dull and dark gray.

Fur Couch stays cool at night, even in summer, and I tend to fall asleep quickly on it. It's like sleeping on a giant animal.

But that night I can't fall asleep. As I listen to dad snore, I watch out the front window, eyes on the sky, and hold the picture of the UFO, waiting to see if it returns. I kneel there for hours. I don't want to leave my post.

When I try to wait up to catch a glimpse of Santa on Christmas morning, I fall asleep right before he shows.

I don't want to screw this up. But I drank three Shirley Temples that day, and my bladder is painfully full.

Around one a.m., I can't hold it anymore. I hobble down the hall to the bathroom, pull down the front of my pajamas, aim for the side of the bowl to keep quiet.

I sigh as the pressure eases. From the side window, I see the neon sign in the tinted bar window is on. Bright and flashing. The words COLD BEER flick on and off inside a red oval.

A red oval!

I do a double take as the UFO makes its appearance.

My stream swings, hits the rim, splashes on the floor and my feet. I pull up my pants. Cover the piss puddle with the bathroom rug and head back to Fur Couch. Dad will be angry about the piss mess, but I don't care.

I run my hand over the fur. Black then gray. Black then gray. I don't have trouble falling asleep this time.

An hour later, I'm woken by a strange humming sound outside the window. Except it's not really a sound but more of a feeling that thrums inside me.

When I sit up and move the curtain, I see a disc-shaped spaceship hovering just a few feet away. A drawbridge-type door lowers, and blinding light pours from within. All warm and inviting.

I look back into the dark apartment. Hear my dad snoring. Then slide the window open and climb out.

Transition

The sun is low,
peeks through treetops that are
beginning to show spots of red and yellow.

Hummingbirds have headed south again,
and we watch out for
foraging black bears
whenever we go outside.

Autumn is here.

Night Music

three a.m.

Frogs, toads, and insects send a disjointed rhythm through the valley. Like an out of time band of old, bow-legged men playing washboards, spoons, and mouth harps.

Since the surgery, I've spent nights in the living room, reclined in a zero-gravity chair as it prevents me from contorting into awkward, regrettable positions during my narcoleptic slumber and aggravating an already frustrating recovery.

I smoke some pot in the kitchen bathroom. Decide to hold off on another oxy dose and sit back in the zero-gravity chair, maybe read a book or flip through the television menu but not watch anything. Or maybe I'll just listen to the bow-legged old men play their washboards, spoons, and mouth harps.

Choice

My eleven-year-old son called up from the basement to tell me there was a mouse in the mousetrap.

I went down with a green plastic bag from Caraluzzi's and found it upside-down on the cracked concrete. One front leg was clamped.

The mouse stared at me with black, bulging eyes. Quivering whiskers. I picked it up without releasing the trap and placed it in the bag.

"Can I see? Can I see?" my five-year-old daughter asked as I put on my wellies.

I opened the bag and both kids peered in. It was a sad sight.

"What are you gonna do with it?" my son asked as though he dreaded my answer.

Living in the country, this is a fairly common occurrence. When the temperature begins to drop in autumn, mice come into the house to stay warm, find the insulation within the walls. Usually, the traps deal a quick death. Occasionally, this happens.

I had planned to do what I've always done in this situation, which is to bring the mouse outside and use the heel of my boot, then leave it on the lawn with a pile of stale bread for the crows. They always take the mice first.

I looked at my son. "Well. It's not dead. So, I'm gonna bring it outside." I held back the rest. And felt like a coward for it.

"Can I come? Can I come?" asked my daughter.

"Why don't you stay inside," I told her. "It's raining and we left your raincoat at school on Friday."

Outside, I opened the trap. Released the mouse on a scattering of wood chips where it crouched, shaking with fear and a useless front leg.

As I raised my boot, something made me stop.

I could feel someone watching me.

I turned slightly and, out of my periphery, saw two sets of eyes staring intently from a living room window.

Though I felt morally compelled to end this poor mouse's suffering, I didn't want my kids to see me kill an animal.

Possessed by a sudden bout of wishful thinking, and the very slim chance that this pocket-sized rodent was merely stunned, I gave it a nudge with my toe.

The mouse wanted to bolt but only managed to hobble a few inches.

It was fucked.

I knew what had to be done.

But before I knew it, I had pinched its tail between thumb and forefinger and tossed it into the wet, high grass where it bounced once and disappeared in the green.

In typical cowardly fashion, I chose to save face in the eyes of my children, rather than put an end to the unnecessary suffering of an innocent animal that was merely looking for a warm place to sleep.

Victories

When you've drunk a lot,
like,
way too much, a lot,
and you know you're fucked
come morning,
except you aren't
fucked,
in fact,
you wake up feeling perfectly fine.
No headache.
No lethargy.
No heaving and repenting
over a puke and shit
splattered toilet bowl
while thoughts of suicide swirl in your head.
Well,
at least not *those* thoughts of suicide.

These are my victories.
And I celebrate them
appropriately.

Kitchen Floor

Lying on a kitchen floor. The linoleum cool on a feverish cheek. I remember the feeling well. And when I see my daughter doing it during a recent bout with the stomach bug, the sensation comes rushing back.

I can remember the waves of nausea she's experiencing. Nothing that goes into her stomach stays there. A popsicle holds promise until it is sprayed on the floor as she attempts to bolt off the couch. Unable to make the toilet.

Timing is everything with puke.

She stays home from school again the next day. I don't feel so hot either.

"Can I sit and be sick with you on the couch?"

She glances up from the clipboard where she colors a page from her *Frozen* coloring book. But I receive no answer.

"That's okay. You don't have to speak if you don't feel like it." I move a pile of tissues aside and sink into the too-soft cushions. Her eyes look empty and washed out despite a good night's rest. Her face drawn and pale from lack of food and hydration. Her eyes flick back down. She colors the picture with little stubs she fishes from a tin box of Crayola. Peeling back the paper when needed. She loves to break crayons in half.

My wife is on her way to work after dropping our son off at school. It is nice to sit here quietly with my daughter. No need to say a thing. It is enough to color. Or watch the chilly autumn wind undulate the bright red leaves on the two maples that stand outside our living room window. Not many people can do that; sit without talking.

Winter Guests

They come when the weather turns cold.
Squeeze in through the many gaps and cracks
of our old house.
Stink bugs.
Native to Asia.
Introduced through trade.
We don't squish them.
That would be cruel.
Plus we've heard that's when they stink you.
Even the cat seems to know this.
She'll paw at them but quickly lose interest.
So they fly freely about the house.
Sometimes we catch them in our hands,
bring them to the door,
and toss them out into the cold.
To their deaths I presume.
Which is also cruel.
But for every one that we get rid of,
three more appear.
So there's always a few crawling around
somewhere.
At night the papery sound
of insect wings pass your ear.
The buzz against a lampshade or window
startles you from a book.
My youngest makes these winter guests a place
to live.
Contractor and real estate agent in one.
A box becomes a house.
Bottle caps, spools, and match books transform
into furniture.
She tapes plastic wrap on the windows.
Pokes air holes in the top.

Gives them stuff she thinks they will eat
but never do.
Sometimes the stink bugs escape.
Sometimes they never leave.
Their forgotten husks rattling inside
like a maraca
when we toss the boxes
in spring.

Soda Jerk

When I was at their house,
my grandparents would sometimes give me a can of Coke
to help me come down from all the Mountain Dew
I drank.

One day I decided to
add a little juice to my Coke
from a jar of maraschino cherries.
This gave the drink a red tinge and
was the sweetest
most
delicious thing
I'd ever tasted.

I told my grandparents I'd invented a brand-new drink.
And they let me believe it.

I called this new invention Cherry Coke.
Made it every time I went over to visit.
Tinkered with the ratio of cherry juice and cola
to get just the right balance of flavor.

During lunch at school one day
I was
feeling generous with my
culinary discovery,
and told one of my only friends.
A cool kid named Michael overhead me.
Laughed in my face.
He said Cherry Coke already existed.

Said it loud enough
for everyone to hear.
I didn't believe him.
So he brought a can to school
just to prove it.
To rub my stupidity in my face.
How could I not know about this?
I watched plenty of TV.
There had to be commercials.
I felt betrayed by my grandparents for not
telling me this.
Someone called me Soda Jerk.
Others joined in.
My face turned red
as the can in Michael's hand.
I could feel the heat in my cheeks.
I tried to lie.
Backtrack.
Convince them it was just a joke.
That I knew about Cherry Coke all along.
But it was too late.
The predators had
surrounded the prey.

Tradition

I stand at the window and watch
two crows and a squirrel
eat yesterday's bread
as cars drive by
the house.

My son hums a
toneless tune
while he makes origami animals
at the kitchen table.

My daughter and wife
are in another room
discussing where to keep her violin
and
what to wear
for dinner tonight.

We will be having sushi.

It might be a
Christmas Eve
tradition.

Sense

Fucking spring.
Allergies.
Humidity.
Ticks.
Snakes in the shed.
Posers on motorcycles.
And ants.
So many ants.
On the floors, in the cupboards, on the ceiling, even
in the toilet, ready
to bite my ass
anytime I take a shit.
You'd think all the spiders in our house would take care of them, but
they just hang out in their webs all day,
waiting for the food to come to *them*.
And y'know I
kinda like the sound
of that.
Maybe they got it
right.
Makes me wish
humans still had the good sense to
take their cues from life forms
much smarter than they are.

Note to Buy an Air Conditioner

The old lady next door dropped dead.

Cooked inside her sweaty apartment
like a Sunday pot roast.

Remnants of a hurricane,
the weather service tells us
and issues a heat advisory.

No hunger, no desires, no
energy for anything except
feeling hot and miserable.

No.

Too hot,
even for misery.

Feelings wilt like weeds and wildflowers
nodding along a dry ditch
that just last week was muddy
and full of chirping frogs.

I listen to the cicadas, now,
as they rev up their engines
but
where did all the birds go? The
squirrels and rabbits?
A fly lands on the deck and is
instantly seared by the white heat.

I try to be still and read,
to stay close to the fan

blowing hot air,
as the toilet tank sweats puddles
on the bathroom tiles
and the doors refuse to close
in their swollen frames for
even they have given up.

Assassin

My grandparents had this
outdoor patio
in the shade of an
ancient tree
and surrounded by hedges.

In summer I liked to
squish the little beetles
that crawled out
from under the slate.

"I squished a beetle!" I'd say
and Grooty would always respond,
"Was it John,
Ringo,
Paul, or
George?"

I never understood the joke
until long after she was dead,

and it's still not funny.

Horses Don't Wear Glasses

He's sensitive to loud sounds. When we go bowling on Thursday afternoons, we bring protection. A pair of blue Vic Firth isolation headphones. Which look comically big on his five-year-old head.

We usually keep the headphones in the trunk of my car. Except this time, they aren't there.

He looks worried.

"Maybe it won't be so loud," I say.

But when I open the bowling alley door, loud music and the sound of balls crashing into pins has him clinging to my leg.

Rather than turn the car around to look for the headphones at home, I go to the closest place I think will have a cheap pair.

The greeter at Walmart stares at my arms as we walk in, uncorks a finger from each nostril and says, "Nice ink," before he plugs back up again.

We find a pair of orange headphones in the hunting section. Next to the camo, ammo, decoys, and guns. The kid points out that they aren't blue. That they aren't his "Vics."

I ask him to try them on, half expect him to refuse until I agree to drive all the way home to search for the headphones he knows.

But he lets me slide the cups over his ears. And after shaking his head to make sure they stay in place, he seems to accept them.

When a salesman in a Realtree cap approaches, I hurry to self-checkout. Once there, the kid won't take the headphones off. Insists on wearing his new "orange Vics" out of the store.

I consider walking out without paying. No one seems to be paying attention. But if I get caught for such a stupid thing, my wife would kill me.

And what kind of example would that set for the kid?

Seriously, what kind of example? It is Walmart, after all.

In the end I scan the sticker on the headband and slide my card through. The receipt checker at the exit doesn't check our receipt.

It's a busy day at the bowling alley. But the kid looks at ease in his new orange headphones. He walks through the front door like he means business.

We rent shoes. Get a lane. Hit the racks to look for balls. The kid picks a pink one with opaque swirls.

People like to talk about all the disgusting feet that share the same pair of bowling shoes. But I can't help thinking of all the fingers that have slipped into the holes of the bowling balls.

Soon, the kid is beating me two games to one, though, to be fair, the little cheater is using bumpers and a ball ramp shaped like a dinosaur.

I mentally blame my performance on my aches and pains. But the truth is I was never any good at bowling, or most other games. I sucked even before the bad back. And I seem to lack a necessary competitive gene.

But today something makes me want to do better.

It just feels like I should be able to beat a five-year-old at bowling.

I consider using the ramp, just to even things up, but quickly reject the idea.

In the middle of our fourth game, me and the kid are neck and neck. My wife would let him win, but fuck that shit. I at least want to tie this up, two to two.

But I fail to hit a single pin while going for a spare, and a lightning bolt of pain radiates from the hardware fusing my L4-L5, extinguishing my rare case of competitive spirit.

A cartoon bowling pin laughs at me on our score monitor, as a dash appears in that frame.

The kid gets up for his turn. Gets distracted by the hand dryer vent on the ball return.

I ease into one of the hard plastic chairs and notice an old couple a few lanes away who have just arrived. Each carry a bowling ball bag. As they settle in, their movements are slow and arthritic, like you'd expect from people pushing eighty or whatever they are.

I watch them tie their shoes. Unzip their bags. Labor with the weight of their bowling balls.

Their arms brittle wooden spindles covered in blotchy tissue paper.

I wonder why they don't find an activity more suited for their aging bodies, like bridge or watching TV, and kinda laugh to myself. They might be the only people in this place I'd stand a chance against.

But everything changes when they hold the bowling balls at chin level and enter their starting positions. Something else takes over.

And they move toward the line like gazelles avoiding predation on the open plains.

Winding up, the dry and crackly old man and his squat, pear-shaped wife each effortlessly throw a leg out behind them.

With graceful little hops, they release their balls. Balls that seem to spin and rotate every which way except according to the laws of physics.

The kid calls for me to watch him. He has a look of intense concentration as he heaves his pink ball onto the dinosaur's back, positions it between the guiding scales, and nudges it down the ramp.

We watch it slowly rumble down the lane in a straight line to connect with the one and three pins, sending all ten down in slow-motion.

Looking like a bobble-head with his headphones, the kid does a happy dance along with the cartoon bowling pin on our score monitor.

I laugh and accept my defeat.

While the kid and his dinosaur continue to wipe the floor with me, I keep tabs on the old couple. It's a game of strikes and spares for those two. Nothing but strikes and spares.

I wonder about their secret—as if there is one—and notice the old man wears glasses with some sort of blinders affixed to the sides. Like what you see the horses in Central Park wear.

The blinders, I mean.

Horses don't wear glasses.

Remnants

Watching home videos
of my kids'
birthdays and school concerts
fills me with
painful longing.

That old life
with rooms full
of people celebrating
seems like the
remnants
of a dream burning away
at midmorning.

Job Squad for Life

As a child, it was easy to
lose myself in the role of hero.

Hours spent
pretending to be a Jedi,
slicing through Storm Troopers with
my lightsaber.

A soldier
invading a village with his army.

Stone Cold Steve Austin
opening a can of whoop ass
on some poor jobber.

Now,
all these years later,
after life did its thing,
those long ago
battles a blurry memory,
it is the others I relate to.

The losers.

The conquered.

The poor jobbers with their back on the mat,
counting those lights while
someone else's hand is raised in victory
and adored,
their t-shirt sales
going through the roof,
thanks to all your

hard work.

Life is funny like that.

Proper

Grunting in bed
from the pain when
I change positions
or do
just about
anything else

like a proper old man.

Mailbox

It holds our bills, our letters, and
catalogs—some as fat as a bible.

It is a conduit for jury duty,
advertisements,
circulars,
and greeting cards.
It brings invitations,
birth announcements,
tax refunds, and
collection notices.

Often
it is empty,
even when it's full.

In spring and summer
ants like to store their
larva inside which
attracts spiders that jump
on my hand as I reach in.

I bought the first mailbox at Home Depot
not long after we moved into this house.
Black molded aluminum with a red flag and
an eagle stamped on the little door.
It came as a kit that included a wooden
post and hardware.
The most economical choice.

Following the placement guidelines of the
U.S. Postal Service,

my wife and son picked a spot for it at the
end of our crumbling driveway.
It was easy to install, just like the box
said.

But easy to install also meant easy to
knock over.

Eventually, perhaps inevitably, our trusty
mailbox was used for batting practice.
Probably by some bored teenagers out for a
late-night drive.

At the time, my
son liked to check the mail when he got
off the school bus.
His younger sister and I would watch
from the window as he
hopped out of the folding doors and
lugged his backpack up the slope to the
curb.
On quiet, windless days, I could hear the
aluminum *thunk* as he opened and closed
the little door.
He was the one who found the box,
walloped out of shape and lying on the
ground like a dead animal
a dozen feet from the post
he'd helped put in the ground.
He was confused and hurt about what
happened
and wept for a long time.
Not because the mailbox was busted,
but because he felt someone had
done something cruel to us.

The real world has a bitter taste
some of us forget
or learn to ignore.
Dulling the edge can be a long and
painful process.

Much like a child's innocence,
the mailbox was beyond fixing, so,
I returned to the store.
There were other sturdier, more
expensive models but
I came home with the
same cheap kit
I'd bought the first time.

This one stood until our drunk neighbor
backed over it with his truck.
Fortunately, he fixed it before we even noticed.
Reinforced it with a rod of rebar
that ran through the post and into the ground.

A few months later, another round of
late-night batting practice loosed this box
from its moorings.
But, thanks to my neighbor
and his rebar,
it didn't go down.
The post now swivels on the rebar and
can spin all the way around,
making it somewhat resistant to that
particular type of vandalism.

More dents have appeared in the black
aluminum since

and
we sometimes find it spun around facing
another direction.
But for now, our second mailbox still stands,
lopsided with a door
that doesn't quite close.

But it does not complain.

Bearing our peeling
and faded house number.

During winter the snowplows
are most responsible for
mailbox fatalities.
To avoid such inconveniences, I see many people
fasten large boards of plywood to their posts.
For the past couple years I have meant to
do the same.
Maybe one day I'll get around to doing it
instead of just writing about it.

Now both kids like to check the box together.
I watch from a window as they approach the curb,
hoping to find a card or package
addressed to them.
Little geniuses without a care in the world.

Except for the moment.

My son cups a hand to his ear,
listens for those quiet electric cars as
my daughter looks left, then right, then
left again.

They return with slightly disappointed
faces
and a single envelope
addressed to me.
A reminder from my doctor.
It's time to schedule my next
colonoscopy.

Shit.

Is it that time already?

Colon Cancer

I'm afraid to go to the doctor.

I'm afraid not to go to the doctor.

The Quack Shack

I watch the receptionist try to run my card through the POS system. Each swipe ends in the same result: DECLINED.

After the first half dozen attempts, I want her to stop. I don't think the machine will change its mind.

"Maybe the account is low," I say through the narrow opening in the sliding window. "I can try another card." I pull a debit from my wallet. Mentally calculate the overdraft.

The woman says nothing. She appears to be new. Short movements. Starts and stops that suggest an unfamiliarity with her surroundings. But she is determined.

A man gets in line behind me. Right away he is making impatient sounds with his breathing. I don't turn to look at him.

"Just a minute," the receptionist says without looking at me. She calls another woman over. Together, they try to get the card through another half dozen times. Each taking a turn to examine the machine. Lift it up off the desk. Look underneath. Run a hand along the wire. Before finally using my other card.

It goes through immediately.

I slide the cards back into my wallet, turn, and

see the man who has been waiting behind me. He had started adding groans to his repertoire of exasperated breathing sounds. He is short. Mid to late fifties. With some color remaining in his wavy hair and a goatee of gray, almost white stubble. He is wearing a denim jacket. His skin is pale and splotchy.

We make eye contact. I expect to see a look of annoyance on his face. But what I see instead is commiseration. I nod politely and take a seat in the waiting area. Leave a buffer of several chairs on my right between me and a thin man decked out in baggy New England Patriots clothing. He doesn't look up from the iPhone he holds sideways in his lap, thumbing at the screen as if playing a game.

This particular doctor's office is housed in what used to be an indoor shopping plaza, where all the retail stores have been turned into medical practices. Each specializing in a different branch of medicine: podiatry, vascular, urology. I am here to see a doctor who specializes in prescribing medical marijuana.

My state legalized the plant for medical use several years ago, and my wife convinced me to sign up for the program. "You're using it anyway," was her argument. "This way it'll at least be legal."

I told her I wasn't sure. "It's kind of expensive. Feels like a ransom."

"You have kids," she said. "The price is worth the guarantee of not getting in trouble."

I've never been arrested for pot. Or anything else. I am not someone who attracts attention. Good or bad. The last time I was pulled over was in the spring of two thousand. And that was for a burned-out taillight. But I could see my wife's point. We didn't have any savings to speak of. The fines and legal fees for even a minor fuck up like pot possession could crush us. That was enough for me.

At that time, there were only a few conditions that would score you a medical marijuana card. Some were fairly serious. I have one of those—the only lottery I'll ever win. Still, I have to show up for yearly evaluations. And they ain't cheap.

I see the same doctor every time. A tall Russian woman who wears dark eyeliner as thick as her accent. Black clumpy stuff that rings her eyes and flakes down her cheeks. Her exam consists of a few questions and a blood pressure reading, performed by draping the cuff *over* my arm, not around, and giving the bladder a few light squeezes. After that she parrots the rules for my renewal: Only for use in the home. No growing. No selling. Keep out of reach of children. Etc.

My visits to the Quack Shack are usually uneventful. But this one time there was a commotion when the doctor denied someone a prescription. One minute, it was all quiet. Then, the door to the exam rooms burst open, and this guy is screaming and hollering that he needs his medication. That he's paid for his visit, and he isn't leaving til he gets his shit. When the doctor refused, he started throwing the waiting room chairs and spit at her. Two big guys waiting to see the Orthopedist leaped on him. Pinned him down until the cops showed up and carried him away squirming in zip ties.

The man in the denim jacket, who had been waiting in line behind me, finishes checking in. Pays his fee in cash. He walks among the chairs. Sighs and shakes his head. The common area of this converted mini mall is used as a communal waiting area for all the practices. Despite the room being spacious, he sits to my left. Leaving just one empty chair between us.

I can feel his eyes on me.

"Can you believe this fuckin' shit?"

He says it loud enough to echo off the high walls. Heads look up from iPhones and magazines. From a flatscreen playing a daytime news show. Everyone except the Patriots super fan to my right.

When I sat down, I opened a book. Jack Reacher was in the middle of beating up a couple thugs running a protection racket, and I was anxious to get back to the action.

"What I mean to say is, what a fuckin' racket this shit is, huh?"

Having my face in a book is usually a good way to let people know I want to be left alone. But this guy isn't getting the hint. He looks from me to the Patriot, who still doesn't look up from his phone. I make a diagonal, non-committal movement with my head. Neither a nod or a shake.

"How much you think this woman makes a day? Each patient paying a hundred and fifty fuckin' bucks! Jeez. And then there's the hundred you gotta pay to the fuckin' state." He throws up a hand. "I mean, c'mon. That's my fuckin' grocery money. They should just legalize the shit all around so we don't have to deal with this."

He's jittery. Makes lots of hand motions as he talks. Crosses and uncrosses his legs. He jerks his chin at the guy wearing the NFL merch. "You must like the Patriots."

The Patriot nods wordlessly, his thumbs tapping away.

"How far do you guys travel to come here?" Disgruntled Man goes on.

"About an hour," the Patriot says, his eyes still focused downward.

"An hour?" Disgruntled lets out a long whistle. "Where from?"

Patriot tells him.

"Oh, man! Isn't there any place closer that can do this shit now?"

Patriot shrugs. "I never thought to check. Just been comin' here for five years cuz it's familiar."

"I've been comin' here five years too," Disgruntled says. "Since it opened. But the ride only takes me twenty minutes. I couldn't do an hour. I know back then there wasn't much of a choice, not too many doctors were doing this, but shit, there's gotta be a place closer to you by now."

He pauses and looks at me. I'm expected to chime in. Unsure if I want this guy to know anything about me, I lie about where I've traveled from. I pick a town at random and he says, "No kidding, I used to live there. Where abouts you at?"

I know I have two options. I can tell this guy to leave me alone, which will make sitting here with him awkward and cause me to feel shitty for the rest of the day even though he's the one encroaching on my space—the result being I'm unable to enjoy my book anyway—or I can close the book, play along for a few minutes, and forget all about this guy when it's over.

I choose the latter. Blurt out a generic street name. Something named after a tree. A street I'm not even sure exists in that town. The Disgruntled Man grunts and nods. Asks if I know so-and-so. I shake my head and for a minute he seems out of things to say.

Across the hall, a patient is called into the podiatry office. An elderly woman uses her walker to pull herself up from her chair. She moves with short, mincing steps. Like she is in a lot of pain. Like she is walking on broken glass. I wonder if she also visits the pot doc. Imagine her ripping hits off an elaborate, skull-shaped glass bong as she watches *Monk* or *Criminal Minds* or something.

The Disgruntled Man looks at his watch. Checks it against the clock on the wall. He cranes his neck at the pot doc's storefront, as if this will allow him to see inside. Maybe he has X-ray eyes. Or cartoon eyes that can stretch from their sockets, angle around door jambs and hallways. But if he does, they're not working today. Or maybe he just doesn't want to expose his secret powers.

Disgruntled slumps back into his chair and sighs. "Jeez. What's taking so fuckin' long. They called and told me they had a fuckin' opening, so I drove right the fuck over. I'm on disability cuz I'm always in fuckin' pain. So waiting isn't good for me." His leg is shaking up and down. He twists in his chair. "Hey. What time are your appointments for?"

"Ten forty-five," Patriot mumbles.

"Ten forty-five," I say.

Disgruntled stops shaking his leg. He makes a shocked face. Grabs the arms of his chair. "Ten forty-five!" Wha—! That's what time they told *me* to come in. How can there be an opening if there's only one doctor and two people are already scheduled to see her at the same time?"

No one says anything.

The door that leads to the exam rooms opens. A patient leaves and the doctor appears in her white lab coat. Thumbtacked above the door are letters spelling out her name. Letters that appear to have been cut out of construction paper by a child. The color long faded.

The doctor looks at her clipboard. Calls out a name in her thick Russian accent. I hope it's Disgruntled she is calling. The Patriot is quiet. The Patriot will let me read in peace.

But it's the Patriot who springs up and follows her through the door.

Now, it is me and Disgruntled. In the next twenty minutes, I learn a lot about this antsy guy. Without having to ask a single question. Like what brought him to this doctor in the first place.

"In oh-three, I had a bad fall down some stairs. Eight surgeries *that* got me." He holds up one arm. "Four here," then the other, "four here. Now I have nerve damage in both shoulders and the doctor says I need a ninth surgery. I told him, 'No fuckin' way, Jose. No more. I'm done with that shit.'"

He tells me he was on Oxycontin for fifteen years. "I used to take a shit ton of it, but now I got it under control and only take two a day. One pill in the morning and one at night. I smoke these oils in between. Got me a nice vape pen that does me good. And if I feel like I might need another pill, I just drink a sixer and that usually does the trick."

At one time he owned his own business. Installing cable or plumbing or something. But his partner bought him out. "I think he was relieved to see me go. My injuries and all." He shifts in his chair, groaning and hissing with pain as if to illustrate his point.

There had once been a *Mrs.* Disgruntled. He'd met her through work. She was a customer. He'd gone to her apartment to install something or fix something and they hit it off. Within a year they got married and bought a house. A couple of kids came soon after. And things were good for a while. He was happy. His business was stable. Then the accident happened. He had to take a lot of time off work. The medical bills dried up their savings and cut into the kids' college fund. Even though the surgeries didn't help he had to go back to work. He had no choice if he didn't want to lose everything.

The Oxy helped.

At first he'd only take one when the pain got unbearable. When one stopped working he'd take two. Eventually he was taking them first thing in the morning. Swallowing two or three every couple of hours after that. His doctor just kept prescribing more. Despite his heavily medicated state the pain seemed to be getting worse.

He tried to hide the pill use from his wife. But she knew. And after crashing his work truck into a telephone pole the marriage quickly fell apart. "It just didn't fuckin' work out." He makes a dismissive wave with his palm.

I kinda feel bad for the guy. But I also want him to shut up. I nod my head every so often out of some idiotic nodding habit I hadn't noticed before. I know I'm just encouraging him with this. So I try to pay attention. Try to stop the reflex before it happens. But I can't control it, it's useless.

"Now I live with my sister," Disgruntled says. "I feel bad for taking up space in her little apartment sometimes but I help out where I can."

I look at the spot where the two guys pinned the other guy down. I consider going off like that. Grabbing a chair. Swinging it at this guy's head. I smile as I imagine it flying off his shoulders and rolling across the floor. The mouth still flapping. No one here today seems like the type to intervene. Hell, they'd probably applaud me.

But I'm no hero. So I press my back into the chair. Fan the paperback on my lap with my thumb. And listen.

I don't know this man's name. Nor he mine. But I know he has trouble sleeping. "I'm up every two or three hours. The fuckin' pain can be so bad I have to get up and pace just to distract myself from it. If I'm hurtin' too much to pace I have to talk it out. I try not to wake up my sister but sometimes I can't help it." He checks his watch. "Man, I really can't wait that long before the fuckin' pain starts getting bad. If I wasn't yapping away at you I'd be going crazy."

This goes on. People are called into other doctor's offices. Every so often Disgruntled seems to run out of steam and stops talking for a minute. Then he checks his watch, shakes his head and says, "This bullshit!" or "This racket!" before going into something else.

I'm getting annoyed. It's as if I can feel the minutes of my life draining away. I wish he'd stop talking and let me read, but I still don't say anything.

Through the big windows, I see a car turn in under the plaza sign and park. A woman gets out. She comes through the glass doors and checks in with reception for the pot doc. When she turns to take a seat, Disgruntled says, "It's gonna be a long wait just so you know."

The woman's lips twitch in a fake smile and she takes a seat far away from us.

Disgruntled isn't deterred. "What time's your appointment for?"

The woman looks up from her open purse. I can tell by her face that she's not happy he's talking to her from across the room. That her choice of seating should make her wish to be left alone clear. But I can also see she hopes answering the question will be the end of it. "Ten forty-five. I'm really late."

Disgruntled lets out a thin laugh. "Don't worry, you're not the one who's late." He jiggles his thumb between us. "We have the same appointment time as you."

This time the woman saves her fake smile and makes like she's looking for something in her purse. A minute later, the Patriot leaves, and the doctor reappears below her cutout name. It is my turn. I think about insisting this other guy go first, but don't.

As I stand, Disgruntled shifts, groans, and wishes me good luck. I nod but I don't need his wishes. Luck has already abandoned me. I will be approved.

Following the doc through the door, I overhear Disgruntled talking to the woman who wants to be left alone. "Can you believe this fuckin' shit? What a racket!"

I am shown to an exam room. The doctor says she'll be right back. She closes the door behind her. In all the years I've been coming to this place, it always looks like it's just been moved into. Empty. I sit on the exam table fully clothed.

And I'm thinking about a bunny I saw on my way in. I was accelerating up an on ramp when, ahead of me, a cottontail popped out of the roadside weeds. It darted across the lane, under the van I was traveling behind, where it did an *Oh-shit-I'm-gonna-die* kinda dance around the tires and, somehow, miraculously, made it to the other side. Completely unharmed.

Then Disgruntled is there. In my mind, I mean. My thoughts. Now that he's not being annoying right there beside me, I wonder if I judged him too harshly. He's just another fuck up like the rest of us. The failed and the failing. Not quick enough or lucky enough to avoid getting run over like the cottontail. Holding on to whatever he can to survive until the next thing comes along to turn him upside down and shake whatever loose change remains from his life across the floor. But I have a family who cares for me. Didn't always, but I do now. Disgruntled has no one but his sister. And from how he makes that situation sound, it's only a matter of time before she gets fed up with him.

I come to when the doc returns. Answer the usual questions, "Yeah, the cancer is still present . . . Yes, the medicine helps with the pain." Etc. Then I hold out my arm so she can drape the blood pressure cuff over my biceps. I listen to the oral recitation of the terms of my renewal, as she squeezes the rubber bladder, and I nod my head. And that's it.

Before leaving with my official papers in hand, I pause and peek through the door of the waiting area to see if Disgruntled is still there.

Return

Twelve years old,
walking through town late one night,
on my way from
one disappointment to another,
it started to snow.

At the park, I
slipped through the hole in the fence,
came out on the basketball court,
and stopped.

The place was
completely deserted.

Without knowing why,
I stood there under a streetlamp,
breath trailing away in the still air,
looking at the thin layer of snow
dusting the blacktop,
so thin the cracks
still showed through.

The air was clean,
crisp,
and so quiet
I could almost hear the flakes falling,
hear them
land
on the shoulders of my coat.

And a peculiar feeling took hold.

A feeling that,

for me,
at that moment,
everything
was as it should be.

I wanted that
moment
to last forever.
And then the moment passed.
Gone as quickly as it arrived.
As if my awareness of its existence
brought its end.
And I went on to face what-
ever little hell
was waiting for me.

There have been other moments like that.
Little breaks in life that make me
want to stick it out. Hang in
through the rest.
And I am grateful for each one.
But I've never forgotten the first time I
recognized it.
The peculiar, warm sense of peace
I felt inside.
Even after thirty-two years
I remember—
this last good memory of childhood—
and return to it often.

Though it is never the same.

NOTES FROM
A WOOD-PANELED BASEMENT

Alan ten-Hoeve lives in Connecticut. NOTES FROM A WOOD-PANELED BASEMENT is his first book. Twitter @alantenhoeve

Some of these poems first appeared in *The Daily Drunk Magazine, (mac)ro(mic), Versification, Selcouth Station,* and via Stephen J. Golds.

Acknowledgments

Many thanks to my wife and kids, Bram and the Riddlebarger family, Shawn Berman, Bud Smith, Poe Ballantine, Nick Olson, Stewart Sinclair, C. Cimmone, Holly Rae Garcia, Chris La Tray, Alan Good, Stephen J. Golds, Zac Smith, Haley Jenkins, DT Robbins, BF Jones, Kyla Houbolt, Beyond Bud Light, and everyone at The Gallimaufry.

More books from Gob Pile Press:

CLIMB OUT YOUR WINDOW AND RUN WITH IT / SONGS FOR THE DOORKNOBS WHO MISSED THEIR TURN by Devin Sams

IN LOSERS' HEAVEN / DOCTOR GOOGLE by Seb Doubinsky & Justin Grimbol

A SETTLED SHIP IN AN OCEAN OF HILLS / HILLBILLIES AGAINST JESUS by Bram Riddlebarger

NO MOON ONLY A SPACE STATION by Wallace Barker (early 2022)

Twitter: @gobpilepress
Email: gobpilepress@gmail.com
Web: www.gobpilepress.bigcartel.com

Made in the USA
Middletown, DE
21 October 2021